A HERO'S LOVE LETTERS
FROM STALAG LUFT III
FOR A GIRL NAMED GEORGIA

by BR Walsh (aka BR Rinker)

For Rhonda, and Ann and Alvan. Thank you so much for your partisicaption in this work. God love you and Bless you for that. Thank you. Lovingly, Regina Rinker April 23, 2009

RoseDog❖Books

PITTSBURGH, PENNSYLVANIA 15222

For more information or to order additional books,
please contact:
RoseDog Books
701 Smithfield Street
Pittsburgh, Pennsylvania 15222
U.S.A.
1-800-834-1803
www.rosedogbookstore.com

ACKNOWLEDGMENTS

My greatest gratitude is for Georgia's excitement and willingness to share this piece of history and of her heart with me. Also, for Paul A. Diedrich, their son, who faithfully drove her to my salon regularly to add to her beauty and to write this true story. Of course, we always drag our families into anything we do, so this is our "thank you" and dedication of this book to Johnny's bloodline and mine.

Edited by Daniel G. Diedrich
Cover by John Christian Jaksha
Computer Help: Matthew Joseph Jaksha
Georgia and John's family: Jon, Dan, Tad, Gigi, Paul
Grandchildren: Jeff, James, Julie, Joey, Jonathan, Jordan, Jenna, Nate, Daniel, Ted, Erin, Ben, Kate
Great Grandchildren: Kay-Leigh, Ana, Jorga, Ava, Elija, Ian
Regennia's family:
Matthew Joseph Jaksha
Kirsten and Kelly Dow; Colton and Kaden
John Christian and Judy Jaksha; Jewel, Joy

WHY I WROTE THIS STORY

This past year I have had the exceptional honor to meet and write about a remarkable family. A family with a dream and the courage to match all they believed in. This is the true story of one American hero whose family migrated to America so they could have the rights and privilege of a dream.

Their dream was not just about self, but a dream that covers you and me every day in every way as long as we are right... morally right.

This one soldier made an effort that cannot be measured. We have made an effort to give you an account...a heavenly measurement of this one American hero's story.

His village of Avon, Minnesota can bask in Johnny's hard-won nobility, courage, and valor. It reminded me of Elijah in the Bible, who was complaining to the Lord how tired he was of fighting for the right all alone. But, God assured him that there were thousands more Elijah knew nothing about.

If you ever believe you are alone in fighting for what is right; it is our hope you will remember this account of one American hero who was admired for his bravery and noble deeds in all humility and care. We pass this true story on to you, friend, with the personal assistance of his loving soul-mate, Georgia.

It's my belief that you cannot read this account without becoming a better person, as I have done.

This is my thank you to Johnny Diedrich, and his family, and his fellow soldiers - who are ready and willing to go out in the fields of war so that you and I might be free. Thank you, Johnny!

Dear Georgia,

My way of living has changed suddenly due to the fact of being shot down on one of our missions awhile back. I am a P.O.W. now. We are allowed only one parcel each sixty days. Certain items are restricted. I wrote Mother a few days ago and informed her what I needed most. But I can receive any amount of letters. Would you please send me some photos of yourself. Say hello to your Mother and family. I wonder just how long it will be before we can go bowling again. I hope by Christmas at least. We are allowed to write two letters and four cards. Missing you.

Love,
Johnny

CHAPTER ONE:

RIGHT INTO GEORGIA'S ARMS

It seemed by now that Johnny had stepped here, stepped there, stepped everywhere but somewhere in the channels of dictates there had been ahead of him in Johnny's life a plan that only nobles dared to dream of. Georgia was to become the biggest part of what Johnny had dreamt of, fought for, and believed in with all his heart.

The bus, an old, established, Greyhound was carrying him much too slow. He was weary from war; from being a prisoner of it. The thought ran through his mind would Georgia and his family perceive that or would he be compelled to put on a veneer of unshakeable strength.

The weight of it all was already heavy on his mind as he imagined going through that war again as there would be a lot of questions especially from his parents. He could envision his high school buddies hitting him on the shoulder in a joshing kind of manner and putting up their arms in a pretend boxing defense as they always had. They would be laughing, cutting up, jumping around, teasing their prized hunting buddy. But Johnny knew he had learned to read behind eyes (probably just as well as anybody in the world as it had meant survival to him).

He could read the pain they shared with their lifelong friend…but there was admiration also written all over them just as it always had been. He knew that is how it would be. But right here and right now even that faint reflections of what he had just experienced would be as an interloper to his weary heart.

He looked around him from time to time acutely searching for changes since leaving the states. There was a slight April breeze blowing against his dusty window that seemed to be nudging the trees to hurry and finish sprouting their blooms for God's summer festival. The birds were singing at the top of their range. He thought *it might be their first song of spring.* Even though Johnny's body was completely exhausted from the confinement, his heart was beginning to roar a new song.

He didn't pretend to know exactly what the birds were singing, but he joined them anyway in a silent tribute to his own soul's survival. He put his head back and adjusted the foot rest, simultaneously pulling the bill of his crisp, new, Army cap over his eyes. If birds could understand and it looked to him as though this particular one did; it would chirp this song:

"In winter's vast cathedral of gothic grace and cold. You are an interruption distracting from the ol' pure rituals"

His heart nearly leapt out of his body with the thought of *how can we bow our heads and sing; you and I, Georgia, the noble hymn of patience when you have whispered "spring".*

I'll bet that is what they are singing as they're flitting back and forth from the top of the trees that seemed reluctant to give up the last traces of their snow white blanket at the top of its branches.

May 25, 1944

Dear Georgia,

Am looking forward to seeing you one of these days, darling. Forgive the repetitions but don't forget your photo. Am still getting along all right. Missing you always.

Love,
Johnny

CHAPTER TWO:

MISSING AMERICA

What a remarkable miracle a welcome turn of events that Johnny had just come through. Yes, he knew he was part of a greater design when in the prison camp at Stalag Luft III he had been busy doing his morning routine of working in the makeshift garden; turning the dirt over in hopes of raising some turnips and greens when he heard what sounded like a Sherman tank. What! Was he dreaming? He bent over a bit as he had always done when he was hunting and called upon all of his trained senses to verify what he thought he had heard and was witnessing.

There, to his surprise, was General Patton in all his glory right in front of him who seemed to be coming in on a cloud of glory. He was the General Patton he had heard so much about; his pearl handled pistol at his side and his glorious Sherman tank. His soldiers began to cut the barb wire fence that had contained them mercilessly for a year and eight days.

The word freedom was ringing in their ears! The soldier next to him yelled out "hot diggedy! Dam Lordy be Jesus, we're free"!!! Another one yelled "mama, here I come". They were scrambling like madmen to pick up their most precious things.

They were told to make a run for the fence, take a break and then be ready to board ship when they heard the call "all aboard for America"!!! There was no emotion revealed from the soldier with this command but he couldn't contain the pride; it was written all over his face.

Johnny, being the leader that he was, first tried to give the men some sense of direction as they were behaving like madmen. But then Johnny's own irrational heart gave way to the wild enthusiasm. He made a frenzied dash to his straw bunk to retrieve, first of all, Georgia's picture and then his letters from home plus another log he had started for Washington. That was all he wanted.

He could see why General Patton was their commander and hero. He paused a minute to observe history in the making. Patton was diligent in delegating orders to the men he had brought with him. Yea! That was a song too. A master song . One soldier was told to search each barrack-like structure and another was told to get each soldier's name and rank on paper. Patton was especially interested in the one who might have made a log.

The rest was a blur as it began to dawn on him that he was on his way home to Georgia. He remembered when his grandfather was happy he would yell out "guttem himmel" which meant happy, happier, and happiest in German. It encompassed and covered the emotion that there were no other words for. And now it was coming out of Johnny's mouth from somewhere deep inside of him. A heaven sent word that meant God in heaven. Gott em himmel (God in heaven).

With Georgia's picture tucked safely inside his poor quality wallet that he had gotten possession of by trading with some young boy that would appear at the fence and wanted to trade for American soap, cigarettes, or candy that had come in by way of Red Cross packages.

Johnny had been putting Georgia's picture in the main frame of that billfold so it could be seen by him and everyone every time he had to open it. At night he would carefully remove it from the billfold window and place her picture on his makeshift table so that every time he opened his eyes there she was in all her glory as close as she could be right now.

It slowly dawned on him that her picture now had a permanent home...in that billfold and in his heart. His lips moved with no help from him; out came "Gottem himmel (God in heaven)" loud and clear on his way to the Liberty ship.

In one flash of a millionth of a second, his mind went from what had he done to deserve this hell to what had made it change into ultimate joy. In his reverie, he thought he had heard a young woman's voice. He pushed up his crisp, brown, new, soldier's cap to check. It was a young lady, tall, slender, with long dark hair wanting to know if the seat next to him was taken but just as quickly changed her mind because of that something she read in his eyes and scripted on his face. The look said "do not disturb as I am not yet where I want to go". Johnny was grateful that she understood so rapidly. He had recognized that young American girls were brilliantly astute; the only thing he wanted now was his privacy; not to be interrupted in his pool of wonderful dreaming. Checking only for changes on his trip he pulled his cap down lower on his forehead. *Now, where was I*, he thought to himself.

The ship's voyage was in one way glorious but in another horrific. First of all, the soldiers had been out pillaging the cellars and gardens for anything there that they had been denied for that long, horrific, year and eight days.

They were told by the people at the fence that there would always be some kind of a dark, home brewed, intoxicant in the cellars that the Germans were noted for. They broke into some of them near their camp. They drank, they danced, and they ate

until they heard the call from the ship "all aboard for America!" Each soldier stopped whatever they were doing in whatever state they were in and for the longest pause placed their hand upon their hearts.

Officers helped gather them up to set sail for what should have been a long, uneventful journey. It was anything but. Approximately mid course across the Atlantic, over choppy seas, it sounded like all the boards would break in two. All that had occurred were the insatiable appetites being overwhelmed.

They thought that was bad but then something worse materialized right in front of them. It was a giant iceberg that brought them to a dead stop and would be adding three more days onto their eighteen day journey that's how long it usually took for a iceberg to painfully pass. Johnny put that time to use trying to figure out what he could invent to make it move faster. The rest of the time he spent holding onto the rail. Like everyone else he lost the food he had tried to eat. By now, he was skin and bones. All of the soldiers' stomachs had shrunk and appeared to be folding back toward the spine.

The ship had been amply stocked with a tremendous amount of groceries and chicken and the soldiers ate like there was no tomorrow. So they would eat and run to the rail and lose it; eat and run and lose it until finally they could hold down what they had eaten. Maybe the glacier was God-sent in that way.

And so we ate, wrote notes, played cards, and told feeble jokes we had to make up ourselves to keep our life force, life strength going. They weren't really funny at all but we would laugh harder at those stories because we understood that underneath our plight we were just a bunch of guys trying to stay alive anyway we could.

Johnny chuckled out loud when he remembered the one about "what do you call a prisoner who can fly through hell but can't break through a dam barbed wire fence"? Everyone would

yell simultaneously with a grin "a country bumpkin" and that one really made us laugh because everyone knew and had heard of the country bumpkin who knew exactly what to do and had already done so and was one of their greatest heroes. Every now and then Johnny would push up his cap, take a quick look for changes along the highway and also to reassure himself that this wasn't just a dream. *I guess not*, he told himself, *there's that girl again.* She wanted to know if he would like the extra bologna sandwich that her mother had thoughtfully put in her overnight case. He politely refused it and pulled his cap back down—all I want is to see Georgia. I need to see her and somehow convey to her how much she has meant to me in my "so- called darkest hour" and if she understands that concept, I want her to know that I desire her to always be in my life in a meaningful manner. She has made a difference in my life that cannot be measured.

The little generous girl sitting across the aisle from him finally realized that this very good-looking soldier was deep in a dream-like state of thoughts and there really wasn't any reason to disturb him anymore. "He makes a very handsome soldier", she told the pleasantly plump lady with a twinkle in her eyes. "Yes," she replied, "he does, in fact". They couldn't keep their eyes off of him. They seemed to perceive he was someone special.

Johnny had made himself aware now only to the bus driver calling out the cities that brought him closer and closer to the one his heart yearned for. He made sure he could hear the cities called out; sometimes loud and clear; sometimes faintly as he repositioned his seat to recline even further back; pulled his cap down to cover his eyes and his nose. He could feel the stares and remarks around him pushing in on his own thoughts.

Oh how he dreaded to deal with the crowd at home; he was war weary. Tracing back over the slow, horrific journey, his mind mulled over the scene just before the ship landed. The view of the American flag waving in the wind and her grand

shores took his breath away. When he caught some air, he and all the men yelled out simultaneously "Gott em himmel". It had become a by-word for all of them to express gut-wrenching emotions.

Across the Atlantic now and right before his eyes was the shoreline of all he believed in. There were hundreds of people waving and shouting and a very young chorus of cadets over to the right of him singing in a controlled, deliberate manner. *"America, America, God shed his grace on thee and crown thy good with brotherhood from sea to shining sea".*

Tears welled up in Johnny's eyes; this time he didn't care who witnessed this gut-wrenching emotion. Swallowing hard, straightening up, pulling his lean shoulders as far back as he had strength. This was for him the perfect moment with only one thing missing. *If only she were here*, he thought. That's what made Johnny a hero; he could give others what he could not allow for himself. He was relentless in those things. He believed in peace and prosperity not just for himself but for everyone.

By now no one bothered this single-minded man intent on getting home and allowed him the space to drift in and out of chaotic sleep. Johnny wouldn't call it sleep. It had been a long time since he had been able to lay his head down and go peacefully to sleep as he did as a child.

Still, as tired as he was, there was a part of him that couldn't let go. Well two. One was the complete rest he was looking forward to upon arriving home again. Two, it was still heavy on his mind just what did Georgia really think of him in the deeper recesses of her soul.

There was an uneasy feeling mixed with the most heightened emotions that he had ever felt; mingled with the anxiety of anticipation. In this half-way dreamy state of sleep he could hear Georgia's "yes" about the letter. He mused that maybe she has another "yes" in her. Maybe, maybe, maybe, maybe.

The next thing Johnny heard was the bus driver announcing his gratitude for those who had chosen Greyhound and for those of you who are terminating their journey here. "This is the city of St. Cloud. We will have a ten minute break here and will proceed on to Avon Lake. Please be prompt and have your tickets ready. Thank you for traveling Greyhound. Thank you, soldier" he added as the tried to digest the words "thank you" that he hadn't heard in a long, long time.

The words Avon Lake broke through his veneer which created an avalanche of new, mixed emotions that made him sit up and take notice. People were dispersing here for their own destination even the nice ladies across from him or maybe they have miles to go. That's the strange thing about life. It was one or the other. Many times we have no idea which.

Johnny knew he understood that but did Georgia know. He was soon to learn and the anxiety was higher than anything he had ever felt before. Deliberately and slowly he got off the bus to stretch his legs and to alleviate some of the anxiety and to his glorious surprise he stepped right into Georgia's arms.

August 6, 1944

Dear Georgia,
According to the latest reports, it takes at least six months to receive mail from home. Hoping to hear from you soon. Am still in good health. Missing America very much.

Love,
Johnny

Chapter Three:

Freedom

Unbeknownst to him, when his father had received word that his son was on his way home and the route he would be taking Mr. Diedrich went immediately over to Mr. Schmid's store to tell Georgia's father and Georgia the good news.

The two of them hatched a plan to beat the townspeople to their hero by meeting him fifteen miles from Avon in St. Cloud. These two men seemed to understand fully the toll that war had exacted on Johnny. Now they were all here. Johnny hadn't, as yet, seen any of the other family. All he saw and yearned for, at this exact moment, was Georgia. Everything in him wanted to grab her, fling her into the air with the delight of a child. Holding back, he gently put his arms around her simultaneously kissing her cheek so as to graze the corner of her mouth with a question and a promise.

Georgia was completely in awe and for a moment it was just the two of them in their magical electromagnetic field. Georgia's arms were like he had felt hundreds of times before in his fantasies but this was even better than he could have ever imagined. Now he had to struggle to keep focused on this world in another way.

It was as though yesterday was now and time stood still. The now that he had fought for. He sent up a quick prayer that his fellow soldiers and friends had a moment like this.

Georgia caught that look in Johnny's eyes and gently brushed away the trace of bright red lipstick on the corner of his mouth. They somehow had to include the rest of the family. They both, like good soldiers, pushed back their emotions again so they would include the waiting family.

September 30, 1944

Dearest Georgia,

How quickly one's pace of life changes. Yesterday and days before were so dull and empty. Today the sun was shining brightly even though the sky was cloudy. Georgia, darling, never have I received such a beautiful letter as yours. It has made this day the happiest I have known as a "Kriegie". One minute you are in your glory enjoying every bit of what American freedom stands for –happiness! As a P.O.W. there is nothing to do but sweat out events, hearsays, and rumors. I Stare through and at the fence, walk within the confined borders, discuss past experiences, and plans for the future. Missing you, darling, more than you know.

Love,
Johnny

CHAPTER FOUR:

THE HAPPIEST I HAVE EVER KNOWN

The soft look on Mrs. Schmid's face told it all. She was witnessing her little girl turning into a young lady right before her eyes. She sighed and looked at George to see if he had caught the transition of their little girl that they had so closely nurtured.

Georgia and Johnny blushed and the men seemed to be speechless; but finally it all gave way to the usual cordials and dividing up in the cars appropriately.

Mrs. Schmid managed to say "how was your trip, dear"? *Oh, there's that word again,* Johnny thought. *This time I will get her two baskets of wall-eye fish out of the lake. Oh, I'll get her all the fish in the lake if she wants them,* he thought to himself as he flashed back to an earlier time when he had first knocked on her door.

This was going through his mind as he slid in next to Georgia who had already gotten in the back of his father's Buick. Georgia's dad was in his new Chrysler behind them. It ran through Johnny's mind *just how many grains of barley would that beautiful, stately Chrysler buy* being the good soldier that he was. *Stop it!* he told himself. *That part of your life is over never to be revisited again. You have now,* he told himself. He had learned that was more important than anything. He and Georgia in his perfect dream.

15

October 16, 1944

Dear Georgia,

Did you send the snapshots yet? Thanks, darling, for writing to me so often! I'm afraid I'll be tied down this year so here's wishing you a Merry Christmas and a Happy New Year!

With all my love,
Johnny

CHAPTER FIVE:

WITH ALL MY LOVE

Yes, Johnny did make it home again. They had all agreed on the trip over to avoid talking about the war. At the same time, they agreed to avoid the crowd in Avon. They understood Johnny knew Avon inside out and could get them to his home indirectly avoiding everyone in town. They would be at the bus station which was a stone's throw away from the Schmid's General Store.

It was too close of quarters on the back road for the new Chrysler but they made it eventually. Really slowing down so as not to scratch Georgia's Dad's new car. It also gave the kids more time to sit together and get reacquainted.

They made it! Each one took their place at the big oak table in Johnny's folk's new home. Well, newer than the cottage by the lake and Johnny had not seen this home as they moved while he was gone. In this home there was actually a dining room. Mrs. Diedrich had put a fresh cotton tablecloth on the table and the ironed, crisp folds were still in it. It smelled so good and just a simple single magnolia in a crystal vase.

Conversation flowed freely now. Johnny wanted to know about his buddies who had signed up with him. Mrs. Diedrich quickly told him about his cousin who had been killed in action. Johnny was really shocked and said what they all knew and that was how happy his cousin had always been. He was fun and full of life he told them as he looked at each one individually.

Before his eyes reached Georgia's eyes, Mrs. Diedrich jumped up suddenly from the table, disappeared around the corner, and before any one could say anything she reappeared with a package about the size of a shoe box but more square. "Here Johnny", she said. "This was sent to Stalag Luft III while you were on your march. For some reason it was sent back to us. We were worried at the time what that would mean but thought we would just wait and see. I think it's from Georgia".

At this point, Johnny's mind was still on his cousin. He felt terrible. He was even more grateful to God that he was able to come home and that he had endured all hardship with God's help. He knew with every fiber of his being with God's continued help he would be able to fulfill his dreams. He wanted to continue to serve his country in some kind of professional manner. That's what he had told the birds and that's what he had sworn to the stars.

October 16, 1944

Dearest Georgia,

If there are more than seven heavens I was in it all day. Talk about sweet letters, Georgia, honey, I received one from you today. My thoughts were laying in a triangular array. Home, Georgia, and how long will it be? Your letter was strictly dessert in the line of brain food and dreams. I drooled at the mouth when you mentioned strawberry shortcake. I went on my first parole walk this afternoon. I was notified to the extent that there was a personal parcel in the outer lager for me. I would get it either Saturday or Monday. No, sugar, we don't hear American broadcasts. Have been spending most of my time reading in the reference library and accumulating material for a wartime log. Tell me about the church celebration. Your letters are everything.

Love,
Johnny

CHAPTER SIX:

CANDY KISSES AND WARTIME LOG

Johnny quickly opened the battle beaten box and there was maybe one hundred candy kisses made of taffy and wrapped in colorful paper. *So appropriate,* Johnny thought. Georgia said

"I couldn't look. I was thinking what did I send him? When I saw the candy kisses I got embarrassed and looked down again. Johnny hurriedly closed the box for me. I could read Mom and Dad's mind saying well that was a good idea". Mom's eyes were sparkling.

Honestly that was the turning point coupled with our legs just touching on the way home that day in the back seat of his family's car. Johnny told me years later he was just thrilled touching my leg. He never wanted the ride to end. It never has and it never will. And so just as in the St. Cloud movie he first took me to we had the same chemistry...it all came flooding back and adding up. Johnny knew now he could ask her. Thank God for candy kisses.

Georgia told me "honestly, that was the turning point for both of us". Johnny also said years later it was the signal to release his pent up flood gates of emotion. *These kisses,* he thought, *would be as sweet as Georgia could be.* A definite signal to him that she did care as much as he did. "I did love him", Georgia told me, "but I wouldn't tell him until he knew me and had the same feelings to want me in his life in a meaningful manner to see if we complimented each other lives".

We were both achievers with high ideals and our faith was the foundation of our lives. Everything was built on faith. We both strove for the good things in life. By us both believing in a higher power it allowed the spiritual journey to unfold and awaken in each of our lives which leads to all that is creative, positive, and good.

Daddy saved us that night at the big oak table saying "well, folks, tomorrow is another day. We have to go home now", he added while he and Mom headed for the side kitchen door which was closer to the car than the front way out.

Johnny walked me to the door right after them but out of earshot from anyone he asked "When can I see you again? I have something to tell you". I said right away without hesitation "Oh, tomorrow you can pick me up at St. Benedicts around 4:00 p.m. after college classes". "All right", he said, "I'll be there".

November 15, 1944

Dearest Georgia,

Each letter from you, darling, definitely brings more and more happiness into my restricted life. My reason for craving snapshots so is for present state of affairs, it is the closest we can be to one another. I hope the sisters won't be too angry with me for cluttering up their main parlor more than their want. What subjects have you taken up this semester? On my return to the states I intend to get my share of walking in the woods, skating, fishing, hunting, bowling, and dancing, if you wish, with you, Georgia, darling, to strains of beautiful, slow, sweet music. You'll have a big job teaching me all over again. I shouldn't be dreaming out loud. The parcel in which you enclosed your snapshots arrived on October 26 in perfect shape. Thank you, Georgia, you are as beautiful as ever. The one of you in the white suit makes me weak in the knees. You may write letters with envelopes if you wish. I'd prefer those to the forms, then you can enclose snapshots. Say hello to everyone. Maybe I'll be dropping in for a visit soon. Bye darling, thinking of you day and night. Don't practice bowling too much!

Love always,
Johnny

CHAPTER SEVEN:

MORE AND MORE HAPPINESS

We were in a booth across from each other by a window that overlooked Saut River. We just had a Coke; that's all we ever drank. We went together to the nickelodeon to choose a song. I think it was the *Shadow Of Your Smile* or it could have been the older version of *Dancing In The Dark*. I was amazed at Johnny's marvelous smooth dancing. He just glided me around the room. I had worn my mint green tailored prom dress with a butterfly sash.

To tell you the truth I wasn't yet thrilled. I wouldn't let go until I knew this was real and that I wasn't just dreaming. We didn't even have to talk because the singers said it all. He kept giving me secretive looks with a new twinkle in his eyes. Finally, we sat down and I got the courage to say "Johnny, you said last night that you had something to tell me. What is it"? I said without being coy, unable to hold the question back any longer. He looked down into his glass and rolled the remainder of the Coke around as though he was trying to read tea leaves. He looked at me with a very serious look and said "I have to go on a train to Santa Monica for rehabilitation. Will you go with me"? I cupped my head in my hands and began to cry uncontrollably. He looked crushed. "Why are you crying"? he asked.

"Oh! I'm so happy"! I said. That was the moment I realized I could let go.

That night we drove home in complete silence. The music was in our hearts now. He walked me to my door and gave me the warmest, most precious, kiss that spoke of forever. Johnny's dream had been planted in my heart that night. That dream is still alive and growing. It will never end.

So in that first kiss Johnny gave me after his proposal to me in the form of "I have something to tell you" was wrapped the promises that any girl could ever hope to cherish and in my colorful wrapped taffy kisses; I didn't realize it at the time but they would turn out to be my promise to him as sweet and as glorious a future as I could help make it.

I honestly can't remember if he kissed me in his car or after he walked me to my father's door as everything faded away but his warm, passionate kiss that spoke of forever coupled with a sweet mystery yet respectful and full of trust as I felt him let go in my small arms which opened the floodgates of my soul and I returned his love by kissing him back. Now, I understood what a real kiss was; just what real was.

Needless to say, I was totally mesmerized. Just the thought ran through me, just as he would have gotten Mom all the fish in Lalee Lake; I would now go anywhere just to be with Johnny...anywhere.

November 8, 1944

Dearest Georgia,

I've been thinking of you all day wondering how many days will pass before your next letter will arrive. Make it soon, darling. As for the latest town hall movies it will take months to catch up on them. Send me a list.

Love,
Johnny

CHAPTER EIGHT:

MAKE YOUR LETTER SOON, DARLING

As fate would have it, we had to get through ten long months of preparation for our future. It was a trying thing to do when all our senses just longed for each other. All we really wanted was to be together; to console each other; and to make up for the dark, dark year and eight days of Johnny's confinement when we were literally snatched out of each others arms but not our dreams.

Some visions die hard if they ever do. By now I was a Junior at St. Benedict College studying Liberal Arts and loving every minute of it. My Mother had the seamstress come live with us as she did the fittings and sewing for my wardrobe. Beautiful suits and formals were being made for every affair. I do believe that Mom was living her life through me. I also believe I became so committed to finishing my education; realizing the weighty investment my Mother and Father had in me. Mother had relinquished her own worldly concept for my Father and traded them off for the higher road. She saw herself in me.

One time they took me to the Minneapolis Auditorium with my new three-tiered, light green dress on with a butterfly tassel around my waist. I was placed up front being the youngest pianist; I was only 11 years old then. There were ten concert grand pianos on stage. I was lost in my playing of Brahms but the photograph had captured that moment and that picture appeared in the Minneapolis Tribune the next morning with great reviews. Mom would brag and show the people who would listen in Dad's store but they didn't seem nearly as impressed as Mom was or maybe it was surprise I read on their faces.

But it was that wonderful night with the auditorium packed that I became fully aware of that respect and admiration; the thing my Mother wanted to achieve one way or the other. I couldn't help but think even as a little girl *this is what every human being should be shown*. But I have to admit to you that Johnny's kiss topped even that as there really aren't any words for an emotion like that; one that will carry one through to eternity. Not even "guttem himmel". What I do remember is what Johnny said at the door in the light that Dad had left on "I'll see you tomorrow night". I, without thinking, asked him if he would pick me up at 4:00 p.m. at St. Benedict College. He, too, without hesitation, said "I'll be glad to".

With the exception of the one month in Santa Monica, thus began our ten month long pattern of seeing each other after our busy days. I was grateful that Johnny allowed me to fulfill my promise to my parents. We both understood they just wanted me to be able to have the illustrious career with or without them. That would give them and us the peace of mind we all deserved. I felt it was up to me as my sisters were more interested in the arts. Their investment in me was huge. Mother's even more so!

To Johnny's credit, he could surmise all of these issues going on inside of me but still he gave me a choice. I could go with him for his rehabilitation; a mandatory obligation on his part as a soldier. It was scheduled in Santa Monica for thirty days. I was in tears as I told him I wanted to go with him but I couldn't go to Santa Monica. I would marry him but not right now. He looked at me for more explanation and asked "Why"? When I revealed to him that I had made a promise to my parents to finish my Liberal Arts training his look softened and he said "All right".

That was the awesome thing about Johnny as it seemed that anything that I ever did or said was just all right with him. He always seemed to take great pride or delight when I would express my wants; my needs; and especially my "I feel I have to".

December 13, 1944

Dearest Georgia,

It is surprising how difficult these letters are becoming to write. Yet it shouldn't be that way. If it wasn't for your sweet letters and especially the snapshots, I'd go berserk. They afford me the only real happiness I have here. My log book is done as it ever will be. So when a good book comes into the room it makes the rounds of the Sergeants we now have. Our life here is simply an opportunity for and development. Every moment spent reading is sort of

The other day we started an inter-room bridge and pinochle tournament. Kes and I are in bridge. Did I ever mention that we took first place in the volleyball tournament in the Sergeants League? We are planning to do the same in basketball. This afternoon we were very fortunate winning our first game this season. I know that bearable best, darling, but please send a photo of yourself as soon as possible. I have a very special reason! Missing you, Georgia, more than you know.

Love,
Johnny

CHAPTER NINE:

AM I AN UNBEARABLE PEST

Johnny had things to do. Also, he always felt he had "miles to go before he slept". He began by seeking out each high school buddy and personally thanked them for being there for and with him. He did this with fervor, knowing so few of them were left.

Sometimes he would go alone to his secret hunting places. He'd try to sing or whistle a tune with delight. His old dog, Rusty, was faithful and true and would always oblige him an ear. In these spots deep in the woods of Minnesota he would take great care to explain to Rusty where he had been and why. He'd always end with "Rusty, we have a great country and we have to protect it. I would do it all over again for you, my family, my country, my friends". Rusty never moved. Rusty seemed to understand every word as Johnny just kept talking and chewing on a twig.

Little by little his nerves began to subside as he had his evenings with the girl of his dreams. I played in Mom's parlor for him on my baby grand piano. Out of the corner of my eye I was always watching him. He would sort of stretch out and put his head back as strains of Brahms would drift through the house mixing with the wonderful smells of Mom's kitchen. She somehow knew that beef pot roast with vegetables and a bay leaf was his meal of choice and would cook that meal often. Johnny knew Mom loved fish so he would sometimes bring all the fish he caught that day with his friends to Mom. Needless to say, we ate very well.

As the time was drawing near for Johnny to go to Santa Monica, he was wrapping up odd jobs he was doing around town. Johnny asked me to go to Avon Lake to pick out our engagement ring. Again, we didn't talk all the way over which was 15 miles and all the way back. He said "Georgia, get what you really want. Don't worry about the price". Even though I was struck by that, I picked out a simple, wide band. I wanted the world to know that I had been caught. I couldn't help but be reminded of birds that I had seen in sanctuaries after they had been caught; they always seemed quite satisfied to me. Birds always played a role in our lives together…actually a prominent role. I could not wait to be banded by my Johnny and then, I was! Again, there was no need for words but we did love looking at each other and we did that often.

December 21, 1944

Georgia Dearest,

Your last letters arrived on Thanksgiving Day. Hope to receive a few before Christmas. We are supposed to receive special (Xmas) Red Cross parcels. Bud received a cigarette parcel tonight from his wife. Thinking of you always, darling.

Love,
Johnny

CHAPTER TEN:

THINKING OF YOU ALWAYS, DARLING

In Santa Monica, Johnny said they were put up in the Santa Monica Hotel on the beach. The best of everything was there for them. He could look out his window and see the other soldiers playing games and running wildly in the sand. It was just their way to relieve all the pent up emotions. Johnny had already done that in the woods of Minnesota with his loyal dog, Rusty, at his side.

Here, still he had thinking to do and chose to stay close to his room and plan his and Georgia's future together.

Given he was missing her more than he could say, that month seemed almost as long as the year and eight days that demanded they put their love on hold again for God and country, family and future. Still, Georgia wrote him a letter or a note every day to keep him abreast of things happening around Avon and in her heart.

By now Johnny's main concern had become her heart—of filling it with the most beautiful and wonderful expression that a man could ever give the woman he loved. He had to adamantly will himself to quit watching the clock and the calendar. "Here, guys, take these to your labyrinth. I'm exhausted from watching them. Maybe you can make better use of them" he said as he slowly removed his watch and gave it to his fellow soldier. He had seriously considered throwing it out the window; he grinned to himself...to watch time fly by he mused.

But in some astonishing twist of fate, time had become his friend. It was no longer a howling, raging wolf at his door that sought to devour all he believed in; to eat at his very soul as though he had never existed. But for the still, small voice in the marrow of his bones always reassuring him "Johnny, you can do it with God's help. We've instilled in you the power to do so. The light must not go out". In his greatest silent moments that whisper would always modify his great trials.

Still, it was with brut force that he went to the dinner table in the elegant dining hall. He knew it would help him and the others to regain what they had lost. He also understood the most important and healing part was to think of his fellow soldiers...the team. So downstairs he would force himself to go. He would manage to muster up a kind of a grin coming into the beautiful room. As soon as he heard the music (the same songs Georgia had played for him) and saw the soldiers eating so well plus each one had put on their best clothes, best behavior, too, he would think...*so who's the leader now.*

He would soon break into a great big smile and mingle a bit but none of them wanted to hear dumb jokes anymore. As soon as he could find his way clear and everyone fully occupied, he would quietly escape back to his room, his picture of Georgia, and fall into the most wondrous sleep. It was the kind of sleep that spoke of tomorrow no longer the yesterday he had made himself so feverously cling to not long ago.

February 20, 1945

Georgia Darling,

We were very fortunate today. I received another letter from you. So will write you immediately. A notice was read to us at appell this evening to the effect that we have personal parcels and mail coming in soon. It is the most wonderful bit of news we have had for a good spell. Also, a German daily paper came in. Trying my best most of the day to translate it. I wish Mother would have told me there would be days like this. I read your letters over each night. Comparing your and my day. Swearing to myself now and then that I will do everything possible to make up for the past ten months. All we have to cling to now are our memories. I imagine it will be very boring listening to my hubba-hubba when I return. But that will be our sweetest moment to set foot on the states. Hope you don't mind this sentimental letter. Under the present circumstances, no choice.

Love always,
Johnny

CHAPTER ELEVEN:

SWEARING TO MYSELF

Finally back home; it was a chilly night with a full moon when Johnny decided to change the pace for Georgia from going to her house every night for dinner and basking in her beautiful concert piano music in her Mother's parlor; so afterward, he suggested they take a ride up to Sleeter Hill.

The thing he wanted to share with Georgia was the beautiful romantic view where this particular night they would be able to see seven cities from the very top. It would be the perfect after dinner drive; the perfect night with the full moon and full stomachs. They had binged on the walleye fish that Johnny had hitherto given to them and Mrs. Schmid had sprinkled with her own special seasonings and rolled in a cornmeal mixture and baked to perfection. A drive and a walk should have been the perfect thing. Also, not to mention the panoramic view. The scene was spectacular and seemed to play on every emotion deep inside them. There were very few words spoken that night. The radio was on and the songs said all that was needed to be said. They were wrapped in a divine presence that could not be described. It was hard to interrupt this perfection but Johnny was aware of how Georgia's family would feel. With that in mind, he reluctantly tried to start the engine on the blue Essex he had just bought and he was trying out. At the same time kind of sharing it with Georgia with great pride. He reached to turn the key on, heard a click, and the engine died. Johnny tried again and again. It was strange. It really didn't bother us. We just stepped outside and once again basked in the moonlight. That moon had long since become his friend he told Georgia. Our hearts were full. We didn't really want to let go of the beautiful panoramic view that spoke of our future together that kept me from becoming frightened in any way and after all I was with a hero. There were cities sparkling like diamonds below us; a hint of our life to be.

In that beautiful moonlight I was as still as I could be. I did turn toward Johnny so that I could read his face and he said "Georgia, tomorrow is another day". My father's words...words he knew I would understand completely. I could see the outline of his smile in that moonlight moment. It's a moment that still nudges my memory constantly and puts me right back on Sleeter Hill; that perfect moment wrapped in forever with Johnny.

We both decided at the same time that we had better start to walk. We knew it was about five miles home and that Mother would not rest until she knew we were home safe. As we walked along thank God we didn't need to talk for in the shadowing distance we heard a group of men exchanging expletives. They seemed to be upset about something. Each man carried a rifle on his shoulder. Johnny nonchalantly reached down for a long stick and put it on his other shoulder. I'm sure in the moonlight it looked just like a hunter's rifle.

I didn't ask questions; I just walked trying to keep up with his highly trained pace. He told me later that it was beginning to remind him of that Nuremburg march. I waited until the last minute but finally had to admit to Johnny that my feet were freezing. He didn't hesitate at all to begin to fashion out a seat for me with pine needles. He told me to sit down; he sat down facing me then he reached for my feet taking my shoes off and he began to rub my feet and open his shirt and gently put them on his warm chest. It didn't take long for me to become comfortable after such an affectionate gesture as that and I stayed comfortable all the way home.

When we finally arrived home it was wonderful to see the lights on. Mom remained in her room though; she knew there was no need for questions as she trusted me implicitly.

At breakfast when I told her what had happened she said she knew something was wrong and couldn't sleep until she heard the door open and my footsteps heading down the hall to my room. I remembered thinking as I turned off the lights *my world has changed drastically and I like it.*

That was our last drive up Sleeter Hill but our favorite thing to do was to take long drives anytime we got a chance on the lower roads. Many times the radio wouldn't play when we were out of range and I would try to break our long silences by telling him stories of my childhood.

It was surprising to me how much he had observed about my life since moving to Avon. He said sometimes he could feel someone watching him. Then, he would add with a grin I thought it was an angel but then you are one. He didn't really tell her then but he was thinking O*h my darling troubles heaven in her goodness. Wells of kindness are in her eyes. Her soul speaks to me. I listen and the strings of my heart respond. The birds sing and we dance in harmony to the musical sound of heaven.*

Johnny wasn't going to let any one particular incident define who he was. He understood clearly that it is the lightness or darkness that emanates from ourselves or the warmest or coldness that says it all. So not only did the world have its hero but Georgia did too.

Our families came together when Johnny's grandmother arrived from Europe and they met at St. John's Abby. There my grandmother said to Mrs. Diedrich "You are welcome to live with us on our farm until St. John's church finds you a homestead".

Strangely enough, Johnny and I did not know this fact until after we were married. We just naturally fell in love. I loved him the first time I saw him when I was only eight years old and I found out later he was ten years old.

When I wasn't doing concerts and practicing my piano and cello for events in and around Avon; formal or informal, I really enjoyed being a drum majorette for a ninety piece state champion band. It was something that seemed to pull us all together. After our wonderful comfortable silence was established, I began to open up and share with Johnny about my childhood in Avon and my family's role in its development. I could remember a little bit when it was just a bunch of cut down trees. Then little by little, the roads were carved in and the town part defined. It was first called Spunk Lake and then Avon Lake. My father built the bar and restaurant and began buying other businesses.

Our schooling, our long talks, and drives made the ten months to my graduation and then the wedding fly by.

I seemed to have the perfect childhood and it took me years to realize that many others did not. One of my fondest memories that always makes me laugh was the time my sister, Joy, and I were left upstairs of the store while Mom and Dad went to play cards with the neighbors. In our freedom and boredom I decided to take the scissors to Joy's beautiful long ringlets. She didn't like them anyway. I thought I was being articulate and artistic. Mother and Dad vehemently disagreed!

Chapter Twelve:

The Perfect Dream

Our wedding was held at St. Benedict's church. Dad hired a photographer from the St. Cloud Times to take wedding pictures at the church and at the banquet at the St. Cloud Country Club.

After the ceremony he tried to capture the kiss when we came out of the church door. Somebody said "How could Johnny kiss you with all those lilies in front of your face"? Then he did manage to get a good shot of us when we got into the car. We were on our way to breakfast to dine in my Mom's Queen Anne dining room where our attraction had begun. Then at 1:00 p.m. we headed for the country club for the wedding dinner. All of my aunts and uncles and Johnny's relatives were present.

This was the first event held at the country club after the war because it had been closed for the duration of the war.

My sister Mary's girlfriends were to be servers at the meal. I really can't remember what was served. My Dad had taught me to think conservatively so this was my bright idea of saving a little money until one of the girls tripped and spilled beet juice down the back of my gown. I couldn't see it so I just overlooked the incident. It wasn't a level of detail I was concerned about. I think my Mother would have been concerned but Johnny always seemed to know just what to do so he danced with me in the corner where all the flowers were placed from the church ceremony. It worked out perfect. No one ever knew. It was a glorious day!

My grandfather and grandmother, Frank Sr. and Gertrude Schmid, and Johnny's grandmother, Louise Diedrich, were so happy to be posing for pictures after our dinner almost in disbelief that they were coming together for such a happy occasion.

They told us they had never seen such a wedding and celebration such as ours. The priest that performed the ceremony had known me since birth. He christened me and was now giving me to a hero that he had also known for a long, long while and respected. After he married us and with the toast he teased Johnny a bit by telling him he knew he had good taste when he had bought his old Model T and he added "don't forget, Georgia and Johnny, the "T" stands for trust". Then he tapped our glasses. We all drank to that. Thinking back now there seemed to be embedded in him the ability to make all my days glorious.

Before the wedding we took our folks to dinner. Johnny wanted to ask my father for my hand. I hadn't told my Dad anything but Johnny had forewarned his folks. Johnny said "Mr. Schmid, I would like to take care of Georgia in marriage for the rest of my life. Would that be all right with you"? It looks as though all the blood had drained out of my father's face but he managed to nod his head until a "yes, yes" finally came out. I'm sure he was thrilled he just wasn't quite ready to give up his little girl.

For our big day, June 1, 1945, my Mom had hired a popular chef to come to our home and prepare a wedding breakfast. We were served scrambled eggs with bits of chili pepper in them, French toast with powdered sugar and a touch of cinnamon sprinkled on them with real maple syrup. What really was vivid still in my mind were the expertly cut grapefruit so each section was exactly like the next and a beautiful cherry on top boiled slightly and piles of crisp bacon and dark German coffee.

After this grand breakfast we then proceeded to the country club that had not been used since the war. It was a grand affair. Dad had pulled some strings to get it reopened like only Dad could.

On the way to the club we had to pass my college so I said "Oh Johnny could I just introduce you to my teachers". They were in the middle of a pageant but there were four nuns on the balcony on their way to join the rest of them. They seemed really pleased with Johnny and asked me to wave at the others gathered for the pageant. There I stood in my wedding dress with the long train and bell wedding cap waving as calmly as I could in all this excitement. I said "Johnny, I wish I had some more flowers to throw". We looked at each other and grinned remembering how my best friend had jumped to get my flowers at the church. In my heart it was her I wanted to catch them.

At the country club I was still pretty much dazed. I'm glad for that beet juice on my dress would have bothered me greatly. Still here even with the nuns partly because of the nuns all felt I had been touched by heaven.

We actually couldn't wait to be on our way. We drove all the way up north to the Duluth Hotel. Johnny rented a room on the eleventh floor but not until he showed the desk clerk our marriage license. He smiled at us. I felt myself blush.

We stayed there for three days so we could go sight seeing on the sand bar lake. After we left there we drove up the Lake Superior shoreline all the way to the Canadian border. Then stopped to watch a huge waterfall that falls and falls again. It was spectacular!!!

Next, we found ourselves in a beautiful white birch bark tree forest. The smell of fresh knotted pine in our newly built cabin resort relaxed us completely. Johnny said "why don't you put on your two piece bathing suit. I'll build a fire and we'll roast hot dogs on the beach". The little town only had one store and they were out of hot dogs. They told Johnny only the Spam was left. We both said at the same time that will be all right. We just stuck a stick into the thick slices of the meat and held it over the fire and slightly burned it on the edges. It was delicious! When our hearts were full and running over we forced ourselves to turn back toward home.

Johnny had surprised me with a beautiful black laced negligee the first night away from home. I wore it briefly for him. Mother had sent a beautiful pink one and a white one. We liked the pink one best on me.

Johnny's mother had sewed his new pajamas feet and sleeves up so he sat patiently undoing her wit.

We next checked in at the Sheraton Hotel in Minneapolis. The same place I had played in concert with the ten concert grand pianos on stage. I was so glad that no one knew me this time.

That night Johnny took me to a gigantic pagoda style restaurant in the heart of the city. We had heard of its excellent reputation even in Avon. I was handed a menu that was almost as big as I was and I was lost. Johnny leaned toward me and said "honey, why don't you try the frog legs; they taste just like chicken only better" and he was right.

From there we drove on home eager to tell our families what we had seen and heard. One of the teachers freely gave us their cottage for the whole summer. We would sleep on the sun porch so we could hear the water lapping up on the shore all night followed by the dance of the wind and the willows on our walls. It was a time there are no words for. "El Natural"

In the fall we both had to think about school. Johnny enrolled at St. John's University as a business major. I had one more year left toward my Liberal Arts degree.

To be closer to our schools we decided to move upstairs above Johnny's parent's home. It was closer than my parent's home and we had three rooms to run around in. When we weren't doing those things we were going for long drives in all directions but never up on Sleeter Hill again. We had to decide what we wanted to do. Johnny's father wanted him to work at the bank so he could travel but Johnny had his sight set on Denver, Colorado "the most beautiful city in the world" he told me.

He told me also "I will go there for a month. I will get a job and a place for us to live". That's exactly what he did.

A month later he came back for his family, packed us up in one day; drove straight through to Denver; our forever dream had been established just as Johnny had said long ago.